Rapid Grammar Series

# Leah at a Zoo
## Book 7:
## A, An & Some

Written by G. Grafi
©2021

A note to parents and teachers:

This is the seventh book in the Rapid Grammar series. Its purpose is to allow learners to acquire basic structures in English. Specifically, this book's focus is on "a", "an" and "some".

Each book in the series is unique in that it allows learners to gradually learn each structure along with basic, content specific English vocabulary.

Refer to the grammar and vocabulary guide on the following pages. Then read the story with your child.

Dr. G. Grafi

# A, An, Some

In English, every countable noun must contain a number in the form of words.


a=1          a book

"a"  is followed by words that start with a consonant sound.


an=1     an apple

"an"  is followed by words that start with a vowel sound.


Some is used for more than 1 and it can be both countable and non-countable:


Some (countable)=1+

some apples

Some (non-countable)=1+

some water

animals 

monkey 

frog 

elephant 

butterfly 

turtle 

alligator 

fish 

lion 

owl 

duck 

bear 

iguana 

rabbit 

whale 

snake

Leah has **a** pet monkey.

Leah's monkey is **an** amazing animal.

Where is Leah's pet monkey?

Leah's monkey likes the zoo.
Maybe he went to a zoo.

Leah will look for her pet
in some zoos in the city.

Leah went to a zoo in the city to find her monkey.

This is the first zoo in a big city.

Leah sees **a** frog.

But she doesn't see **a** monkey.

Leah sees an elephant.

But she doesn't see a monkey.

Leah sees **some** butterflies.

But she doesn't see **a** monkey.

Leah sees a turtle.

But she doesn't see a monkey.

Leah sees **an** alligator.

But she doesn't see
**a** monkey.

Leah sees some fish.

But she doesn't see a monkey.

Leah sees a lion.

But she doesn't see
a monkey.

Leah sees an owl.

But she doesn't see
a monkey.

Leah sees some ducks.
But she doesn't see a monkey.

Leah sees a bear.
But she doesn't see
a monkey.

Leah sees **an** iguana.

But she doesn't see **a** monkey.

Leah sees some rabbits.
But she doesn't see a monkey.

Leah sees **a** whale.

But she doesn't see
**a** monkey.

Leah sees **an** umbrellabird.

But she doesn't see **a** monkey.

Leah sees some snakes.
But she doesn't see a monkey.

Leah sees **some** monkeys.

But she doesn't see her monkey.

Do you see a monkey?
Do you see Leah's monkey?